SUNDAY SCHOOL

Attendance Boosters

165 Fresh and New Ideas

Group

Incredible things will happen®

SUNDAY SCHOOL ATTENDANCE BOOSTERS
165 Fresh and New Ideas

Visit our website: **group.com**

Contributors
We'd like to thank the following people who contributed their creative ideas and hard work to this collection.
Tim Baker, Dr. Robert J. Choun, Karen Dockrey, Monica Kay Glenn, Debbie Gowensmith, Stacey Haverstock, Michele Howe, Jan Kershner, Trish Kline, Kelly Martin, Marilyn Meiklejohn, Todd Outcalt, Christina Schofield, Amy Simpson, and Cheryl B. Slater

Credits
Editor: Julie Meiklejohn
Creative Development Editor: Linda A. Anderson
Chief Creative Officer: Joani Schultz
Copy Editor: Pam Klein
Art Director/Designer: Jean Bruns
Cover Art Director: Jeff A. Storm
Cover Designer: Alan Furst, Inc.
Cover Illustrator: Laura Blanken Merer
Computer Graphic Artists: Pat Miller and Tracy K. Donaldson
Illustrator: Dana C. Regan
Production Manager: Peggy Naylor

Library of Congress Cataloging-in-Publication Data
Sunday school attendance boosters : fresh and new ideas.
    p. cm.
  ISBN 978-0-7644-2153-2
   1. Sunday schools. I. Group Publishing.
  BV1521 .S86 2000
  268'.6--dc21

                                                99-059238

18 17   16 15
Printed in the United States of America.

Contents

ENTICING ENVIRONMENTS

7

ONGOING PROJECTS

33

PARENTS PLUS

59

CREATIVE COMMUNICATION

75

Foreword

Building attendance is a two-part challenge. First, you have to make the Sunday school experience appealing enough to attract new attendees, and then you have to keep 'em coming back.

There are obstacles standing squarely in the way of meeting these goals. Many potential attendees are too young to get to Sunday school on their own; they must depend on transportation and encouragement from adults. Some children are ex-attendees who have reached fifth or sixth grade and have concluded that Sunday school is for babies and nerds. Many other potential attendees are children whose parents have cut ties to the "faith of their fathers" and are shopping around for any church with ample parking.

THE PERSONAL TOUCH

Let's deal first with the hurdle facing those too young to take themselves to church, even if they want to go. Children can be brought to church by adults other than their parents, but a major goal of the ministry of Christian education is to build families, so we need to concentrate on getting the whole family to church. Adult churchgoers can make a habit of inviting unchurched friends, neighbors, and relatives to accompany them to church. In a society in which people are increasingly isolated from one another, personal relationships are a valuable commodity. A flashy Christmas program might get visitors across the church threshold, but friendships are what will keep them there. Consider the example of Christ on the road to Emmaus (Luke 24:13-35). Our Lord Jesus did not airdrop form-letter announcements of his resurrection; rather, he came in person to talk and walk with people who needed reassurance and direction. Membership in the family of God is our goal for the unchurched (and thus every member of the family).

COMING BACK!

To keep children coming back, teachers must realize that teaching the *child* takes priority over teaching the *lesson*. The best attendance builder of all is a loving teacher. Model Christ's love. Make church a place where lasting friendships are nurtured. Paul wrote to the Christians in Thessalonica that he and Timothy shared "not only the gospel of God but our lives as well" (1 Thessalonians 2:8). Teachers who know what their children's daily lives are really like are in a better position to teach lessons their students can relate to.

A child will keep regular attendance if he or she is actively involved in the learning process. Offer children opportunities to take responsibility for their own learning. A good teacher takes the time to pose interesting, age-appropriate questions, provide resource materials, and offer just the right amount of direction and guidance. When a child has a stake in a particular lesson, that child will more easily retain what he or she has learned.

What if a visitor does not return? What if a regular attendee's appearances become sporadic and then nonexistent? Some reasons are out of a teacher's control. Perhaps the family moved. Maybe the visitor's family was just "trying on" the church and found a better fit elsewhere. For whatever reason, a child has dropped out. Concerned teachers can encourage attendance with notes, phone calls, and visits, but they cannot force a child to attend. Children belong to God and his church, not just to your congregation.

SHOW YOU CARE

The best thing you can do is to maintain a friendly relationship with all children—both those with sporadic attendance and those who are regular attendees. Don't let children get the impression that they are cared for only as long as they show up and drop their offerings into the plate. Two perceptions that will dramatically affect a child's attendance are (1) nobody cares if I show up, and (2) nobody cares if I drop out. If the disciple Peter had been in your class and had pulled a stunt equivalent to the denial of Christ in the courtyard of Caiaphas, would you be anxious to welcome him back? Probably not. Jesus, on the other hand, maintained the relationship, initiated reconciliation, and redirected Peter into a lifetime of fruitful ministry. I doubt if I would have even sent Peter a note and a handful of take-home papers.

As you consider the attendance builders in this resource, remember that church growth is not just measured in numerical terms. We are called to the Great Commission, but we are also called to disciple, and discipleship is more than a weekly head count. Religion in America has been described as a mile wide and an inch deep. Let's pledge ourselves to draw others to our Lord by demonstrating and sharing the joy of life in him. Let's commit to helping others become rooted and built up in Christ.

Dr. Robert J. Choun
Professor of Children's Ministries, Dallas Theological Seminary

Introduction

"I can't wait to go to Sunday school!" "I love Sunday school!" "I have so much fun in Sunday school that I'm going to be there every Sunday!"

Wouldn't it be great to hear these things from all the kids in your church? As a Sunday school teacher, you're committed, dedicated, and loving. You work hard to make your lessons fun, exciting, and meaningful. But sometimes you wish you could find ways to reach more kids for Christ and to keep them coming to your class on a regular basis.

Sunday School Attendance Boosters is designed to help you do just that. It's packed full of wonderful and varied ideas to help attract kids to your Sunday school program and to keep them coming back for more. There are tips in this book to fit all age levels, budgets, and time constraints.

One way to make sure kids want to come back to your class is to provide an environment in which they feel safe, loved, and stimulated. "Enticing Environments" will give you some great ideas to help make your classroom a better place and to help you become a better teacher.

If kids have ownership of a project that is designed for long-term learning, they're much more likely to return to continue the work on the project. "Ongoing Projects" has many super project ideas that take place either as a part of your lesson or as a supplement to it.

As we all know, most kids won't make it to Sunday school without an active commitment on the part of their parents. In "Parents Plus," you'll find tips to help parents (as well as other members of the church and community) get involved in your program in many different ways.

Kids almost never receive their own mail, e-mail, or phone messages. "Creative Communication" provides some fun, unique ways of communicating the benefits of Sunday school attendance to both children and their parents.

Now you've got the tools to build your Sunday school program: You have the love for Christ and for children, some additional resources, and the passion to share the Lord with others. So let these ideas boost you into action!

Enticing Environments

What's the first thing children notice when they walk into your classroom? Chances are, it's not your quality lessons or great Bible knowledge. Children get a very quick sense of what they can expect to happen in your classroom from the environment they can see and feel the minute they walk in the door. The environment of a Sunday school classroom consists of many different things, from the actual physical design of the classroom to more intangible things, such as a teacher's attitudes and actions. The ideas in this section will help you to make all aspects of your classroom environment exciting, safe, and Christ-filled.

Share Time

No matter what the lesson is about, invite the children to show and tell something about it each week. For example, you might say, "*Show* me a way you will live this Bible truth." "*Tell* me a good thing that happens in your family." "*Show* me by bringing something special from home that reminds you of God's love." "*Tell* me a way a brother, sister, or cousin is humble."

Sometimes you can ask the children ahead of time to bring things to class. Other times, have them draw pictures of what they would like to share. The goal is to get children to express their understanding. Children will want to come back to a place where the teacher wants to hear what they think and feel.

Attention, Class!

Help kids stay interested in your lessons by letting them do a little teaching themselves. Create several teaching assignments that will rotate each week. (Letting your class help create these assignments will give them more ownership of and enthusiasm for the idea.) For example, you might create the role of Reader. At the end of class, tell the Reader what next week's Bible reference will be, and let him or her read it over during the week. Then the following week, the student can read the Scripture or present a summary of the story to the class. Giving children a definite reason to return next week may just help them develop a pattern of regular attendance!

Lending Library

Many churches have libraries, but they don't usually include many books that would be of interest to children. With the support of your church and the parents of your children, start your own library of children's books, videotapes, and magazines. Allow kids to check out items on a weekly basis.

Surprise!

Build a surprise into each week's lesson to keep kids coming back for more. The surprises don't have to be elaborate, and they should not be tied to performance or attendance. Instead, they should just be fun little perks that show your class how much you care about them.

Consider these ideas:
- a simple snack, such as cookies or fruit;
- small trinkets that tie in to the lesson, such as tiny crosses or stickers;
- pictures of the kids taken with an instant camera;
- surprise visitors, such as the pastor, the choir director, or parents; and
- mini field trips, such as visiting the nursery or holding class in the fellowship hall or kitchen.

With a little imagination, you can build a surprise into each lesson—or at least into every few lessons. Kids will never know what you have in store, and they'll want to come back to find out!

Teasers

Each week, provide a clue about the next lesson. Your clue might be in the form of a snack or something to take home. This will build curiosity about the coming lesson and encourage regular attendance. Here are some examples:

- Two pennies: the story of the widow's mite (Mark 12:41-44)
- Tuna sandwiches for a snack: the story of the feeding of the five thousand (Matthew 14:13-21)
- Apples as a snack: the story of Adam and Eve in the garden (Genesis 3)
- Pumpkin or sunflower seeds: the parable of the sower (Matthew 13:1-23)
- An adhesive bandage: a story of Jesus healing the sick (Matthew 9:27-34)
- Tissues: the story of Jesus crying for Lazarus (John 11:1-37)

Music Time

Find a variety of children's instruments such as a toy drum, a tambourine, and other rhythm instruments. Have kids play the instruments and sing for a few minutes before beginning class or at the end of class time. Most kids really enjoy making joyful music together.

Pleasing Paperwork

To help keep kids connected from week to week and eliminate hassles and headaches when a child is gone for a week, keep a colored folder for each child. You might want to let kids decorate their own folders at the beginning of the Sunday school year. Keep the folders in a box or drawer that is easily accessible by the kids. Then put any information you shared during class—such as handouts, letters to parents, or other information—in the folders for kids who weren't in class. That way, children will be able to access the materials easily. You might want to have all of your kids put their paperwork in the folders each week. Then they'll have a record of the whole Sunday school year to keep.

Conflict Resolution

As kids grow older and become involved in more activities, they begin to have more scheduling conflicts on Sunday mornings. This makes getting them to Sunday school more and more difficult. But who says Sunday school has to be just on Sunday? Brainstorm other possibilities with the kids in your class. Maybe you could meet on a weeknight at someone's house, or maybe Sunday afternoons would be better. If you strive to be sensitive to kids' time constraints, they're much more likely to attend your class.

Big Wig

This is a fun (and funny!) way to keep your kids involved. Each week, bring in a funny hat, wig, or other head covering and pass it around at the end of the class time. Kids will love getting to "cut up" with the funny hats. Each week you can build on the humor by bringing in a different head covering. This brief moment of shared laughter can transform learning into fun.

Poster Mania

Visit your local Christian bookstore and ask the manager if you can have a few music posters. Stores receive hundreds of these each year and are usually glad to give them away. Hang these posters on the walls of your classroom. You might also want to give them out to class members from time to time.

Show Your Stuff

Keep kids coming to Sunday school by creating opportunities for children to participate regularly in the church service. It's not necessary for the children to actively participate in the church service every week, but you'll keep their interest as long as they're always *preparing* for the next time they participate. As part of the church service, kids might sing, recite memory verses together, share what they've learned in Sunday school, or make presentations (such as gifts, crafts, or verbal affirmations) to their parents or church leaders.

Note: This is also a great way to attract parents to church.

Rules of the Road

Kids want to be in places and situations where they feel that their opinions are valued and important. They also want to be treated with respect both by their teacher and by the other members of their class. Begin your Sunday school year by establishing several "ground rules" of respect that all members of the class will commit to following. Some examples might be listening to what others have to say, respecting others' opinions even though they're different from your own, and keeping private things private. Have kids help come up with these rules, and post them in your classroom.

Critters

If you want to attract children to your class, plan to include a few animals—especially pets such as kittens or puppies. You'll find that these furry creatures can lead into wonderful discussions about God's great creation, our responsibility to care for God's world, and the nature of God's love.

Puzzle Search

Photocopy two lesson visuals. Paste one on blue construction paper and one on red construction paper. Cut both pictures into the same number of pieces, and hide all of the pieces around the classroom. Be sure there are enough pieces for all of your kids. As children trickle in for class, place a red or a blue sticker on each child's hand, and tell kids to search for the pieces that match the colors of their stickers. When all the pieces have been located and the puzzles have been put together, the visuals will help preface the lesson. This activity gets children immediately involved, which can help ease the anxiety of saying goodbye to parents. As children work together, they will develop friendships and familiarity that will make for an easier return the following week.

Chair Prizes

Tape a simple and inexpensive prize to the underside of each chair. Prizes may include stickers, dimes, pieces of gum or candy, bookmarks, erasers, WWJD bracelets, pencils, or small toys. Give children time at the end of class to find and remove their surprises. This gesture will remind them of the fun they've had in Sunday school.

Buddy Teams

Help children feel more comfortable and at home in your program by having them form buddy teams. A buddy team should consist of two or three children whose job it is to look out for one another for a certain amount of time—a month or a quarter, for example. Initially, kids can choose their own buddies. As new children join the program, try to pair them with buddies who have been coming for a while. Then be sure to create new buddy teams often so children get to know everyone. Tell children that buddies can greet each other, play with each other, work on projects together, and learn together. Being buddies doesn't mean children can't play with friends outside the buddy team, but it does mean that buddies should be included. Encourage children to ask their buddies to return to the program.

Private Prayers

Some children may not feel comfortable praying aloud, let alone asking for prayer in public. Provide a safe and private place for your kids to make their prayer requests known to you. If your children know that at Sunday school there's one person who really cares and who will pray for them, it can make all the difference in their lives.

Make several copies of the "Pray for Me" form (p. 15). Explain to kids that you'd like to pray for them during the week and that you have a form they can use for their prayer requests. Go over the form with your kids, and emphasize that they don't have to sign their names if they don't want to. Have a stack of the forms sitting out each week so kids don't have to ask for them. Hang a large envelope on the wall, and encourage children to place their prayer requests in the envelope. Then start praying!

Pray for Me

My name is _____.

Please pray for me about _____

_____

_____

_____

_____

_____

I would ❑ would not ❑ like my prayer request to be shared with the class.

Pray for Me

My name is _____.

Please pray for me about _____

_____

_____

_____

_____

_____

I would ❑ would not ❑ like my prayer request to be shared with the class.

Caught in Kindness

Challenge your children to catch one another doing acts of Christlike kindness and to report these to the class. Kids will want to come to hear who acted kindly the previous week, and they'll strive to be kind in hopes of getting caught. Challenge kids to catch each other at church, at home, on the ball field, and at school. Add your own reports to the kids' reports, and keep a tally so you make sure to catch every child at least once. Be kind yourself in hopes that students will catch you!

Awards and Rewards

To help children feel that Sunday school is a warm and affirming place, give out certificates at the end of each month. During the month, be on the lookout for children's special qualities. For example, some kids are kindhearted, some are good helpers, and others like to help clean up. Keep mental notes on each child's special abilities. When you have a good idea of what you'll award each child, photocopy the "You're Special!" certificate (p. 17) on nice paper, and make up a certificate for each child with his or her name and outstanding quality on it. Then at the end of the month, schedule some time during class and give out the certificates. Have the class applaud for each child.

Making the Friend Connection

Many children dislike school because they feel they don't "fit in" with the other kids. Many children avoid Sunday school attendance for the same reason. Create a comfort zone for kids to fit in with your students by helping them make the friend connection.

As children arrive, write their names on slips of paper and put the names in a hat or a basket. Then let each child draw a name.

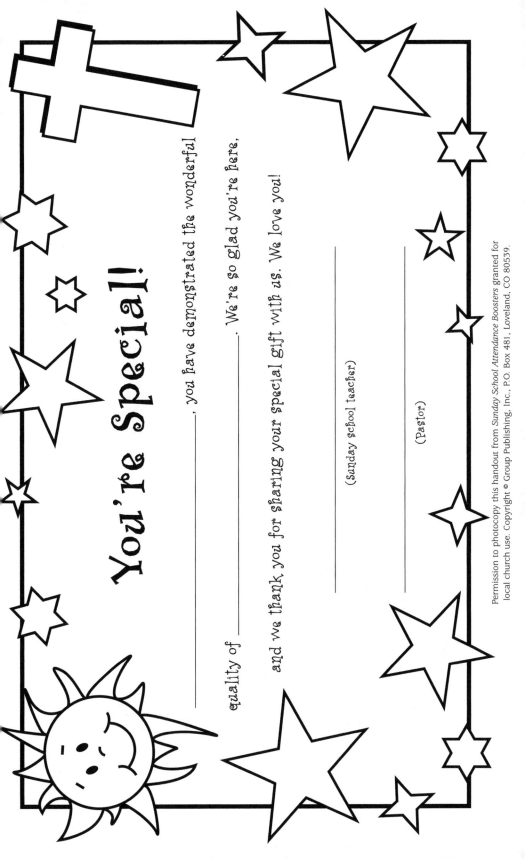

You're Special!

_____, you have demonstrated the wonderful

quality of _____. We're so glad you're here,

and we thank you for sharing your special gift with us. We love you!

_____
(Sunday school teacher)

_____
(Pastor)

The person whose name the child drew will be his or her friend for the day. Begin the class by having partners interview each other to discover a few things the rest of the class might not know. Then have each child introduce his or her partner to the class, telling the things he or she discovered in the interview. Let kids draw new names each week and repeat this activity. That way, kids get to know everyone in the class a little better, and no one will feel like a stranger or outsider to the class.

Birthday Bash

At the beginning of the year, make a list of children's birthdays and schedule them to be celebrated on the various Sundays of the year (celebrate as close to each child's birthday as possible). Send a postcard or letter to those children whose birthdays you'll celebrate on a given Sunday. This will increase excitement, make each child in the class feel special, and will help boost attendance throughout the year. Be sure to keep the birthday celebrations brief, including a song, a birthday cupcake with a candle, and a card signed by the rest of the class.

Bill of Rights

As we are working to share spiritual truths and the love of Christ with the children in our Sunday school classes, we need to ensure we're meeting those children's basic needs as well. When a child feels safe and welcome in a Sunday school classroom, he or she is much more likely to return. Photocopy the "Bill of Rights" handout on page 20 and post it in your classroom. You might also want to give a copy to each child.

You Are Here

Focus on first-time visitors' experiences to encourage them to come back. Welcome visiting families with special visitor parking spaces. Direct visitors with clear signs indicating classrooms, the worship area, and the restrooms. Appoint a greeter to share information with visitors and to introduce children to their Sunday school teachers.

My Name Is...

The most important word to any child is his or her own name. Kids will feel welcome and important if you spend time at the beginning of the school year helping kids learn one another's names. Try this fun name-learning game. Have kids sit in a circle. Go around the circle and ask each person to introduce himself or herself to the class. When everyone has been introduced, challenge kids to repeat everyone's name in order as quickly as they can.

BILL OF
Rights

As a child in this Sunday school class, I have the right to

- ...a teacher who remembers my name and uses it often.

- ...a teacher who shows he or she cares about me by getting down on my level to talk to me.

- ...a classroom that is clean, comfortable, and child-friendly.

- ...enough supplies on hand so I'll know you wanted me to be there.

- ...a fair and consistent plan for discipline. Please explain the rules to me before I break them.

Just My Style!

To keep your class time exciting and fresh, provide activities that cater to a variety of learning styles. For example, some children learn best verbally, so they will enjoy activities involving creative writing and discussion. Other children may learn better with learning experiences that engage the whole body. Make sure the methods you use in your class are interesting, age-appropriate, and fit the aims of the lesson.

That's My Job

Group projects are a great way to help kids learn to work together. Some examples of activities that work well as group projects are dramatic presentations, research projects, discussions, or art projects. Design group projects so that each group member has a well-defined role, and help all group members develop ownership of the group task. For example, in a discussion group, one member might be the Reader, one might be the Recorder, and one might be the Encourager. Group work not only promotes regular attendance, but it also provides invaluable opportunities for kids to practice social skills.

Popcorn Sundays

There are certain foods that kids crave—and popcorn is one of the easiest and tastiest to be found anywhere. Many churches find that industrial popcorn poppers (the kind used in movie theaters) are excellent investments since they can be used for many different types of gatherings, including Sunday school classes. You'll get a boost in your attendance if you advertise special "Popcorn Sundays." Be sure to have plenty of popcorn on hand, and enjoy!

Where's My Teacher?

Regular attendance should be modeled by Sunday school teachers. Seeing a familiar face at the classroom door makes a child feel secure. Young children, especially, need the reassurance of recognizable adults and regular routines. A commitment to teaching for at least a quarter provides wonderful opportunities to get to know a group of children well.

Who Was That?

Anytime you have a child visit your classroom, ask him or her to fill out some basic information on a 3x5 card (see the following example). Keep visitors' names, ages, addresses, and phone numbers on file so that you can stay in contact with them. For example, you might periodically send announcements of upcoming programs or study topics that might interest them.

Welcome, New Friend!

My name is _____.

My parents' names are _____.

My address is _____.

I am _____ years old, and my birthday is _____.

My telephone number is _____.

Attendance, Please!

It's a good idea to keep a record of attendance every week. This will help you to note those who are attending only sporadically or who have stopped coming entirely, so you can focus special attention on them. Attendance records also help chart projected growth for long-term planning, including budget setting, classroom assignments, and curriculum orders.

Cubbies

Help keep your classroom tidy while helping children feel like they each have their own space by assigning each child a "cubby" to place his or her things in. Stack cardboard boxes or plastic crates along one wall to use as cubbies. Help kids feel even more at home by allowing them to decorate their cubbies. Give them paper and crayons and let them write their names or draw pictures. Then help them tape their creations on or near their cubbies. You might even want to encourage children to bring things that remind them of home to keep in their cubbies.

Family Picture

Take a "family picture" of the children in your class. Tell children in advance which day you'll be taking the picture so they'll be sure to attend Sunday school. You might even want to send a reminder note home to parents. Then have the picture enlarged and framed, and hang it in a prominent place in your classroom. Have additional copies made and inexpensively framed, and give one to each child. To help visitors feel welcome, keep an instant-print camera handy and snap their pictures at the beginning of each class. Next to the framed family picture, create a "New Additions to Our Family" sign. Tape new kids' pictures under the sign, and encourage children to be present for the next family picture. If your class tends to grow rapidly, consider taking a new family picture every quarter.

Tag 'Em

To help students remember one another's names at the beginning of a new Sunday school year, have students create their own nametags. There are many different types of nametag possibilities, such as wooden circles to be hung around kids' necks with yarn, cheap baseball caps that can be personalized, or plastic pin-on nametags.

Obtain enough nametag materials for everyone to make one plus several more for visitors. Set out the nametag materials, crayons, paints, colored chalk, stickers, and markers. Designate a place in your classroom for kids to leave their nametags as they're leaving class. This might be a nail to hang them on or a basket to set them in. Encourage kids to wear their nametags for the first few weeks. After a few weeks, have kids try not wearing their nametags and see how many people's names they can remember.

Toddler Tape

Use masking tape instead of nametags for young preschoolers. Write each child's first name on a strip of masking tape and put the strip on the child's back. This way, the child's name is easy to see, and the child won't be able to reach the tape and choke on it. Parents will appreciate that you want to know their children and call them by name. To save class time, prepare name tapes ahead of time.

Puzzle Helpers

Kids love to help! Encourage their natural desire to serve and boost your attendance at the same time. Once a month, make a list of kids who have missed a meeting or two. You'll need one index card for each child. Write a job a child can do on each index card, and cut each card into two puzzle pieces. Make sure that no two cards are cut in exactly the same way. Put one piece of each puzzle in a basket or box in your classroom and mail the other piece along with an invitation to attend Sunday school to each of the kids on your list. In the invitation, tell kids that in order to find out what their special jobs are they need to come to Sunday school. They'll love finding the matching pieces to their puzzles!

Cereal Time!

Instead of having a mid-class snack, designate the first activity as snack time. When kids arrive, direct them to their choice of a cereal treat. Wet or dry, cereal is a fun snack. Stock up on a variety of cereals, plastic bowls, spoons, and napkins. You may want to allow the first few children who arrive in class the privilege of setting out the snack items and serving those who arrive later. Other children might pour the milk, and the rest of the kids might help out on the cleanup crew.

Toddler Cards

Ask parents to fill out cards for their preschoolers on the first Sunday they come to your class. On the card, include such information as the child's name; date of birth and age; parents' first names; people who are authorized to pick up the child; any habits, special needs, or allergies he or she has; and any other important information. After the first Sunday, laminate the information cards and keep them in a file.

Preschool Safety

Together with a committee of parents and preschool teachers, establish preschool policies that provide consistent safety and security for each child. Print the policies and distribute them to all parents who bring preschoolers. Parents will participate much more regularly in a church that treasures its young ones. Here are some sample policies:

- As you leave your child with the teacher, please say a cheerful goodbye. This assures your child that you trust the person who will be caring for him or her.
- Please come to pick up your child immediately after services so he or she doesn't worry.
- Please leave your child at the door instead of coming into the room. This keeps children in the room from being confused by so many adults coming and going. We want them to feel safe and happy here.
- Please keep your child home if he or she has had any fever for the last twenty-four hours, with or without medication. We don't want to risk other children becoming ill.
- Please let us know any special needs your child has so we can meet them in just the way you do.

Welcome!

Kids need to know that they're valued. If they feel welcome and important, they're likely to want to return. This doesn't mean that they have to be bribed to come to Sunday school. It simply means that they need to know that their presence is important to the adults in the church.

So do the little things that show you care. Make sure your craft supplies are plentiful and in good shape. (Who can forget that wonderful feeling of opening a brand-new box of crayons?) Be sure your play equipment is in good working order. (A deflated basketball can deflate a child's enthusiasm.) And come to class on time. Be there at the classroom door to welcome kids with a smile. (Remember the Golden Rule? Treat your kids as you'd like to be treated.) You'll be surprised at how far a little forethought and care can go toward making your classroom a place kids want to be.

Maybe a Makeover?

You may be the best teacher in the world and still feel that you're not connecting with kids as well as you'd like to. Take heart! Your frustration may have nothing to do with your teaching style. Take a look around—is your classroom the kind of place in which *you'd* like to learn if you were a child?

Create an inviting, stimulating environment and soon you will have a classroom filled with happy, learning kids. Ask yourself the following questions: Is my classroom large enough for kids to interact in comfortably, or are kids crammed together with no room to play? Are my classroom walls painted in bright, cheerful colors, or do they look drab and dingy? Do I have fun, informative posters and maps on the walls, or are the walls blank or covered with "grown-up" information? Is there plenty of room for kids to stretch out on the floor rather than sitting up straight in hard-backed chairs? (This *is* Sunday school, but it doesn't have to *feel* like school!)

To make any needed changes, you may need to enlist the help of your Christian education director or your pastor, but the effort will be well worth it!

Making the Grade

This idea may feel a little risky, but the information gleaned could make a huge difference in your Sunday school attendance—*and* in the way you teach! Consider letting kids give their teacher a report card. Not only will you discover how you're doing as a teacher, but you can also evaluate the effectiveness of your lessons.

Give kids a series of questions to answer at the end of each quarter. These evaluations might include questions and statements such as the following:

- Rate your teacher on a scale from one to ten (with ten being the best score). Explain why you gave your teacher the score you did.
- Which Bible story did you like best this quarter? Why?
- Which Bible story did you like least? Why?
- What is one thing you've learned about God this quarter?
- If you could change one thing about this class, what would it be?
- What do you like best about your teacher?
- What is one thing you might like your teacher to do differently?

Caretakers

Kids love taking care of living things. Use this simple idea to nurture kids' sense of responsibility and to keep them wanting to come to Sunday school each week.

Set up a small greenhouse or an aquarium (or both!) in your classroom. In a greenhouse, kids can take a few minutes each week to water, turn, fertilize, or prune the plants. With an aquarium, kids can feed the fish; check the water temperature; clean the filter; or add rocks, gravel, or plants to the tank.

Make either idea more special by letting kids become involved at the outset. For example, provide gardening books or books about fish, and let kids decide what to plant or what kinds of fish to buy. If possible, let kids accompany you when you buy the supplies and have them be involved in the initial setup. A minimal investment can mean week after week of involved students!

Update Me

A great way to help kids feel welcome every Sunday, as well as to help you and other class members stay current on what's going on in each child's life, is to start each class with a brief update time. Have kids sit in a circle. Then go around the circle and have each child share anything he or she would like to share about the past week. Encourage other children to listen carefully and be supportive.

Picture Wall

D esignate a wall in the classroom or church that can be deco-rated. Take pictures each week of your kids as they work on crafts or activities, play, or sing. Add pictures weekly to the display, along with crafts or visuals. Encourage children to show the wall to their parents and friends. You may want to hide a special figure or character among the pictures and move it to a new spot each week. Challenge kids to find the character each time they meet, and see if they can point out new additions to the wall.

Team Building

Kids will want to keep coming back if they feel that they're each an important part of the "team." Foster a team spirit by hosting an afternoon, a day, or even a weekend of team building. Provide and lead activities that will help kids get to know one another better, learn to work together, and have fun together! Be sure to end your team-building time with a debriefing discussion. This will help kids understand how they can use what they've learned, both in Sunday school and outside of Sunday school.

Class Cheer

At the beginning of a year or a quarter, help kids feel like they're a cohesive unit by having them work together to create a class cheer or motto that demonstrates who they are and what they want the class environment to be like. When they've finished their cheer or motto, have them create a colorful poster that includes the words they've come up with, and hang it in a prominent place in the classroom. Every once in a while, have kids perform the cheer or repeat the motto, and be sure to have them teach it to new kids!

Terrific T-Shirts

Kids love T-shirts, especially T-shirts that remind them of important events, people, or places. At the end of a quarter or a year, purchase enough inexpensive white T-shirts for every child to have one. Provide fabric paint, and have kids sign one another's

T-shirts. Be sure to have kids include the class and the year on their shirts. You may also want to have them include positive things about each person whose shirt they sign.

A fun alternative to this activity would be to have kids create a logo for their class and have a local screen printing shop put the logo on T-shirts.

Graffiti

Help kids feel more at home in their Sunday school room by allowing them to personalize the room. With the approval of church leadership, designate one wall of your classroom as the "graffiti wall." Provide markers and paint, and allow kids to decorate the wall using original artwork, favorite quotes and Bible verses, and signatures. If necessary, remind kids to keep their creations appropriate and in good taste. When the wall is filled, paint over it and start again. (Take a picture first, if you'd like!)

A less expensive and less time-consuming alternative would be to tape long sheets of newsprint on one wall and allow kids to decorate them.

Suggestion Box

Let kids voice their opinions by providing them with a suggestion box. Cut a hole in the top of a shoebox, and place a supply of scrap paper and pencils near the box. Tell kids that when they think of topics they'd like to study, activities they'd like to do, or fun ways to decorate the classroom, they should write their ideas on slips of paper and put them in the suggestion box. Once a month, check the contents of the box and act on the suggestions if possible.

Before and After Class

Help kids feel that they're welcome in your classroom at any time by providing activity supplies that they can use when they arrive early or when their parents are a little late to pick them up. Some good supplies to have might be coloring books and crayons, modeling clay, and puzzles.

Change of Venue

If kids crave variety, don't overlook the possibility of boosting excitement and attendance by taking your class to a new location. Let the kids know in advance that you'll be meeting in a local restaurant, outdoors, or at a retreat center. Getting out of the classroom and into the world from time to time will refresh both children and teachers and provide new perspectives on God's world.

Ongoing Projects

Kids love to feel a sense of accomplishment because of a job well-done, and a great way to give them this feeling is through long-term projects in your classroom. Ongoing projects help kids feel ownership of their learning, and they also give kids a tremendous sense of belonging. This section presents ideas that range in length from two weeks to an entire year. Some can be implemented as enrichment activities, and others are programs in themselves. These ideas will help you give the children in your classroom a much-needed feeling of continuity and consistency.

Fabulous Friends Days

Take advantage of Valentine's Day and make the Sundays in February "Fabulous Friends Days" in your Sunday school class. Design invitations with a Valentine's theme encouraging kids to bring friends to class during the month of February. Mail invitations to all the kids in your group, even those who have not attended for several weeks (or months). Serve a special snack each Sunday to celebrate the "Fabulous Friends." Prepare a "Fabulous Friends" poster, and have the kids and their guests autograph the poster at the end of class time. A great Bible verse to go along with this theme is Proverbs 17:17a, "A friend loves at all times."

Make Me a Poster

Invite kids to create a poster at home of the concept they've just studied or the one they're going to study. Explain that you'd like to hang the pictures in your classroom. When they bring them to you, affirm each child as you review the good ideas presented in each poster. Display the posters for at least two weeks, and then start a new poster wall. For kids who arrive early to class, have extra paper and other supplies set out so they can create additional posters.

Hooray for Hollywood!

As a culminating activity for a unit of study, have kids plan and film a video depicting the major theme of the study. The production can be as elaborate as you care to make it, perhaps using props, costumes, and a script. Have kids work together to choose a student director, actors and actresses, a stage manager, and a props person. As students are brainstorming and filming, stand back and act as a resource person, stepping in only when kids need your help.

Show the video to the whole congregation as a fun way to show what kids are learning in Sunday school.

End-of-the-Month Fun

Decide on a fun activity or a treat you can provide for your class for the last Sunday of the month. Then make up a clue about the activity for students to guess each week. On the first week of the month, write the first clue on the chalkboard or on a large piece of paper, and ask kids to guess what the clue refers to. Record everyone's guess on the paper. Add another clue each week and have kids guess again. Give the last clue on the last Sunday of the month. See if kids can figure out the activity or treat!

Drama Day

Once a quarter, have a "Drama Day." Advertise this day well in advance and remind kids that they'll be needed to make the drama come to life. Use this day to re-enact Bible stories, or write your own plays that children will enjoy. If you'd like, videotape your efforts and play the drama back before the end of class time. Kids love acting and will learn from the active roles they play.

Photo Partners

Using an instant-print camera, take a photograph of each student in your class. Let the photos develop, turn them facedown, and shuffle them. Allow each student to pick up a photograph. Once everyone has a photograph of someone else in the class, ask kids to take the photos home and pray for their partners each day. You might want to have kids change partners every quarter. As new students join your class, take photos of them too. Have the other kids change partners as necessary so that each new child will have both someone to pray for, and someone else to pray for him or her.

The Board Game

On a piece of poster board, create a board game with up to fifty-two squares. Try to decorate it with a traveling theme. At the beginning of the game, let each child pick a mode of transportation, such as a car, a train, or a boat. Each week that the child attends class, he or she gets to move the vehicle one space ahead. If you want to be really creative, add some special moves for the kids who can't be there every week, such as "move two spaces." You might want to have prizes for kids at the end of the game.

Shower of Blessings

This would be a great activity to use in the spring or during a rainy season. In one corner of the classroom, construct a "cloud." Take some newspaper, crumple it to look like a cloud, and paint it blue with spray paint. Or simply cut a cloud out of blue paper. Cut blue raindrops out of construction paper or poster board. Every time a student comes to Sunday school, he or she gets to write his or her name on a raindrop and tape it to the cloud. When students miss class, you can mail raindrops to the children to let them know they were missed. Tell kids who miss class to bring their raindrops with them to the next class; they can add their raindrops to the cloud then. Let students know that they're part of your "shower of blessings."

Flashlight Mystery

Ask each student to bring a flashlight to class with brand-new batteries. Talk about how Christians are the lights of the world. Tell kids that each week while they are in Sunday school they will turn on the flashlights and leave them on the whole time. When Sunday school is over, the flashlights will be turned off. Tell kids that when their batteries run down, they'll get to hear the "Flashlight Mystery Story." Look up some Scriptures in which Jesus talks about being the light of the world, and write them on separate index cards. Repeat the Scriptures as necessary to make one card for each child. As kids' flashlight batteries run out, take them aside and tell them about the Bible passages. Be sure to give kids the cards to take with them as a reminder of the Scriptures.

Memory Verse Book

This will help those kids who can't be at Sunday school every week feel connected. Get enough notebooks for everyone in your class. Each week, kids will receive some printed form of the memory verse from the lesson to put in their notebooks. This could be as simple as printing the memory verse on a piece of paper with a border around it for the kids to color, or it could be a really elaborate design using a computer graphics program. Maybe the verse could be included in a crossword puzzle one week. Each week's presentation should be a little different. At the end of the Sunday school year, each child will have a book of the memory verses for the year.

Mystery Game

This activity will help build anticipation for your class. Tell your students you are going to play a mystery game. Each week that they come to class, they'll get a new clue in the mystery. The mystery could be as simple as Jesus' resurrection. An example of a clue might be "It happened during a famous Jewish celebration." Make the clues fit the level of your children. If you have a really bright group of kids, make the clues more difficult. For a younger class, make them simple. Have a "Mystery Solution" Sunday when you reveal the solution, complete with treats relevant to the mystery.

Create a Kid

This project will not only encourage children to come to Sunday school, but it will also build their self-esteem. Tell kids they'll be making life-size posters of themselves over the next few weeks. The first week, draw an outline of each child on newsprint and cut it out. Tape the cutouts to a wall with the names of the children on cards near the feet. Each week that a child attends Sunday school, he or she will get to add a feature to the poster. For example, one week a child might color the hair, the next week he or she might make the eyes, and the next week the child might add some clothes. Remind kids to add jewelry, hair bows, hats, or sunglasses. Let them create posters of the way they view themselves!

Baseballs

This would be a fun activity to do during baseball season. Each week as the students come in, have them all sign a baseball. Place the baseball on a shelf for everyone to see. Bring in a new baseball each week for the kids to sign. As the weeks go by, the baseball collection will grow. Let children know that they'll each get to take a ball home at the end of the designated time period. This will encourage them to be there every week to sign a ball. When the number of balls on the shelf is the same as the number of students in the class, place the balls in a bag. Let each child pick out a ball to take home, and then have the child try to find his or her name on the ball.

Advent Calendar

Try this variation on the Christmas Advent calendar. Get a piece of poster board for each child, and write the child's name at the top. Make calendars with enough spaces for all of the dates in the Sunday school year, and put one date in each box. Each week that a child comes to class, he or she can place a star in the appropriately dated box. Or if you want to make the calendars more elaborate, have children cut out shapes that are relevant to the day's lesson. Here's an example: If your lesson is about Jesus' resurrection, kids might cut out small crosses and tape them to their calendars. You could also use fabric as the background and pin felt pieces to the fabric. As the year goes on, you'll easily be able to track your children's attendance, as well as have a visual reminder for kids.

Absen "Tees"

Try this one to help remedy a summer slump. Tell your students the class is going to play golf. Have each child decorate a foam cup as a golf hole on part of a miniature golf course. Kids might include miniature trees, grass, and even a sand trap. Each week, mail each of your students a golf tee with a reminder to be at Sunday school. Kids will bring the tees with them and place them in their cups as they come to church. Make sure you have extra tees for the students who forget to bring theirs. Toward the end of the summer, plan a fun day for your class at a local miniature golf course.

Volunteer Coaching

One way to encourage children to come to Sunday school is to get involved in their lives outside the church. A great way to do this is to regularly attend children's soccer games, baseball games, football games, theater productions, and other similar events in your community. A better way to get involved with kids is to volunteer to help coach for or lead such groups. As you build relationships with children and their families, invite them to check out your Sunday school program.

Traveling Mascot

Keep kids coming to Sunday school by starting a "traveling mascot" tradition. Find some kind of mascot for your Sunday school class or program. The mascot should be valuable enough that kids will want to take care of it and keep the tradition going. But it should be inexpensive enough that you can easily replace it if it disappears. For example, you could use a stuffed animal, a T-shirt, a doll or action figure, or even a small bowl of goldfish! If you have a large group, you may want more than one mascot.

Have each child write his or her name on a slip of paper, and put the pieces of paper in a hat or box. At the end of class, draw a name from the hat. The person whose name you draw will get to take care of the mascot until the next meeting. Every time someone returns the mascot, have that person report what kinds of adventures the mascot experienced during the week.

Draw a different name each week until all of the children have had a turn. Be sure to add the names of new students and visitors so they will have a chance to take home the mascot too.

Fun Footage

Here's a fun way to keep kids coming back to Sunday school. Each week, have an adult volunteer take a few minutes of video footage during class. Be sure the videographer captures every child on film at some point. Try to make the footage as fun and lively as possible, and be sure every child will clearly see himself or herself on the tape. At the beginning of Sunday school the next week, show the tape from the week before. Kids love to see themselves on the big screen!

Growing in Christ

Cut simple flower shapes out of construction paper and have children decorate them with crayons, tissue paper, or glitter. Take a picture of each child, cut the photo in the shape of a circle, and place it in the center of the flower. Try laminating the flowers to make them more sturdy. Cut a long section of green string for each flower. The majority of string will be tucked under the back of the flower. Let a tail at the end of each piece of string serve as a stem, and tape the flowers close to the ground on a wall. Each week a child is present, let out a little more string and position the flower higher on the wall. Kids will enjoy watching their flowers "grow" from week to week, and the visual will help them understand how time spent with God helps them grow spiritually.

Attendance Chain

Challenge another class to a paper-chain contest. Throughout the unit, have each child write his or her name on a link and add it to the class chain each week. See how long the chain will grow. As the chain grows and decorates the room, children will be reminded to return and to invite friends.

Growth Chart

At the beginning of the year, have each child in your class make a growth chart. On the charts, kids will mark not only physical growth but spiritual growth as well. Kids will be eager to check their height each month, and marking milestones of spiritual growth will help them see God's presence in their lives.

To begin, give each child a length of newsprint at least a foot taller than the child. Then hang the sheets on the wall, and help kids mark their heights on the sheets. Let children decorate their growth charts with colored markers. (You might want to have a real growth chart on hand to give kids decorating ideas.)

Each month, let kids measure themselves to see if they've grown. And each week, encourage children to mark any spiritual growth they've noticed. For example, kids might note times they've trusted God, stood up for God, or obeyed God.

God's Mystery

Picture puzzles have always been a favorite of young children. This can help encourage week-to-week attendance by supplying a hands-on activity that's coordinated to support the topics of your curriculum.

Find several photos, such as those from magazines, which illustrate an idea to be covered by the curriculum during two successive weeks. For example, for the theme of God's care, you might use photos of nature, animals, or children. Make black-and-white photocopies of the pictures. Try to have a different picture for each child in class, and make a couple of extra copies for visitors. Paste the photocopies onto heavy paper or cardboard. Then cut them into several puzzle pieces.

Place all the pieces of each photo into an envelope and label it with a child's name. The first week, give each child half of the puzzle pieces from his or her envelope. Taking clues from the outline of the images, instruct kids to tape the pieces onto a sheet of paper where they think the pieces belong. Have them use small pieces of tape in case they need to rearrange the puzzle later. Teach the first half of your two-week lesson. The second week, give children the remaining pieces. Have them arrange and paste the puzzle together and then teach the second half of the lesson. Then discuss the puzzle, pointing out how color would have made the puzzle easier to put together. Point out that God sometimes seems like a mystery, but he's easier to understand when we put "color" in our pictures of him. That color comes from reading and studying his Word. Allow kids to color the puzzles in class or take them home to color.

Adopt a Bulletin Board

Set aside one section of a bulletin board for kids to "adopt." Every two or three weeks, have a new pair or trio adopt the bulletin board and decorate it however they wish. They might include family pictures, original artwork, and other items. You might want to have the decorations relate to your current topic in class. Provide supplies such as construction paper, glue, markers, and tape or tacks, and encourage kids to work on their bulletin board before or after class time. When the bulletin board is finished, have the pair or trio share their creation with the rest of the class.

Person of the Week

Create a "Person of the Week" bulletin board in your classroom. Each week, have a different child bring in family pictures and other favorite pictures to hang on the bulletin board. Allow the person of the week to share his or her pictures at the beginning of class time.

I'm Part of the Club

Clubs are a great way to welcome children into the church and to involve them in other programs. Club meetings usually include a devotional time, games, music, and crafts. Club membership lists should be shared with the leader of children's ministry, so that the children's names can be added to the mailing list for announcements and calendars of church activities.

Shadow Boxes

This is a great way to help enrich a multiple-week unit. Cut egg cartons into shadow boxes, each made up of as many compartments as there are weeks in your unit. Give children the shadow boxes, and let kids paint them or color them with markers. Cut drinking straws in half and have children glue them to the backs of their shadow boxes, creating stands much like those on picture frames.

Purchase or obtain small objects that illustrate the theme of your curriculum unit and that fit within one egg compartment. Each week, give children one item to glue into their shadow boxes. Children will be motivated to return each week to add to their shadow boxes. When the shadow boxes are complete, let children practice storytelling by explaining what each area of the shadow box represents. Allow children to take their shadow boxes home, and encourage them to share the story with their parents and siblings.

Sowing and Reaping

In the last twenty-five years, more and more of the American population has left rural living for urban life. Fewer and fewer children have personal experience with sowing and reaping. For this culture of city-dwellers, the observation of the miracle of the growth of a seed is something they may never have experienced. So grow something! This idea can tie in to a variety of lessons and themes, including the Creation and God's daily care of our lives. In addition, it will motivate attendance, as a seed does not grow in a day or even a week.

Give each child several seeds to sow and care for weekly. Create an "observatory" in your classroom and students will return weekly to find out answers to questions such as these: Did my seed sprout? Did the flower bloom yet? How long do the roots on a sweet potato grow in a glass jar of water?

Note: Some plants may require more than weekly care; be sure to check on them during the week.

Continuous Story Time

Have kids each write a story in weekly segments. Their stories could be about what it might have been like to live during the time of the Bible passage you're studying, or they could demonstrate a topic the class is discussing. The first week, kids will begin their stories. The following week, they'll add more to the stories. Have kids continue in this way until the stories are finished. Then have them add illustrations and make them into storybooks. Older elementary kids could read their stories to younger Sunday school students.

Tune in Next Week...

Find a children's video or book on tape that goes along with the theme you're covering during a multiple-week unit. Show the video or play the tape for the final few minutes of each class time. Kids will want to return to find out what happens.

Bible Journal

Having kids write about an experience will help them understand it and remember it better. Create Bible journals for each child in your class (be sure to have a few extra journals on hand for visitors). Make each journal by stapling about fifteen pieces of plain white paper inside a construction-paper cover. Provide pencils, crayons, and markers, and give kids fifteen minutes or so at the end of each class to write and illustrate a sentence telling what they learned that day. Children who finish early can work on decorating the cover. Collect the journals each week. At the end of the unit or quarter, kids will have a record of all the stories they learned about.

Sign In, Please!

Using a large piece of poster board, make a poster illustrating the theme for a multiweek unit. Leave about half of the poster blank. Draw a line down the middle of the blank area, dividing it into two equal sides. Invite the kids to participate as much as possible in making the poster.

Divide the class into two equal groups, and name the groups. Put one group's name at the top of each blank column, and have kids write their names in the appropriate column. Tell kids that they can sign the poster every time they attend class, and if they bring friends to class their friends may sign also. At the end of the unit, the team with the most signatures will be treated to banana splits (or whatever reward you choose) with the teacher, pastor, or other respected adults. To reward the kids on other team as well, let them have a treat with you.

Video Pals

Arrange to exchange class videos with a class similar to your class in age and numbers. Let everyone know ahead of time which Sunday you will shoot your class video. When the day comes, brainstorm with your class what you want to include in your video, such as a song, a memorized Bible verse, introductions, or a silly pose. Allow kids to participate in the actual filming as much as they are able. Send your video to your video pals and eagerly await a reply!

You'll probably need to set up a schedule with your video pals to ensure that videos are exchanged on a regular basis. Your video pals can be another class in your own church, a class across town, or a class across the country!

Calendar Creations

Begin this project in early fall so that it is completed by Christmas. Make copies of the blank monthly calendar on page 49. Enlarge the page so kids can easily work with the calendar. Each week, allot some time for working on a single calendar page. Starting with the month of January, ask the children to design a calendar page for each month. Write the name of the month on the chalkboard for the children to copy. Have kids add dates and days of the week in the appropriate spaces on the calendar. Ask the children to call out ideas and activities they participate in during that month, and write the ideas on the board. For example, for the month of January, kids might say ice skating, sledding, snowmobiling, drinking hot chocolate, wearing warm clothes, and sitting in front of a fire. Next, pass out markers, crayons, stickers, glue, and glitter. Let the children draw, design, and decorate to their hearts' content. At the end of class, set the calendars aside until the next week. At the end of twelve weeks, bring in wrapping paper and wrap the calendars for the children to take home as Christmas gifts to their families.

It's Heavenly!

Set up a card table in the corner of your classroom. On this table, place a piece of heavy cardboard cut to fit the table size. Gather assorted materials such as cotton balls, glitter, tissue paper, cardboard, construction paper, foil, clear and colored plastic wrap, glue, scissors, markers, and colorful confetti. Tell children to think about what heaven might be like, and ask them to create their own version of heaven on the piece of cardboard. Encourage kids to brainstorm and work together. Allow children time to work on the

project from week to week after their regular class work is completed. Keep the project materials handy in a large storage box under the table for easy access. After the display is completed, move it into your church foyer for the entire church body to see and appreciate.

Time for Tea!

Dust off a book on manners and etiquette. Make note of the proper way to extend simple courtesies, such as introducing strangers to one another, seating and serving guests at a dinner table, setting a proper table, folding and placing napkins on the lap before eating, requesting refills, and thanking a host or hostess for a lovely meal. Explain that you'll be teaching some social skills and that you'll treat the children to a tea party at the end of the quarter. Toward the end of each class, have your students gather around the table and bring out any necessary props for your etiquette lesson of the week. After your demonstration, assist the children in practicing the skill you've just discussed. Try it several times. Each week, teach your students a new and interesting social skill. At the end of the quarter, host an old-fashioned tea party complete with flavored teas, lemonade, finger food, and small cakes and cookies. Your students can practice being the perfect "guests" while you serve them.

Paint Me a World

Bring in a wall-length sheet of newsprint, assorted crayons, markers, glitter paints, and stickers. Each week, allot ten or fifteen minutes as art time. Read a short story from the Bible that will spark the children's imagination. Some examples are Noah and the ark, the Creation story, and Jesus feeding the five thousand. Instruct the class to work on a specific story setting each week, starting at one end of the paper and moving to a new area of the paper from week to week. If possible, each child should create different aspects of the story you selected. Or have several kids draw the background, some draw the characters, and others work on buildings. After each class, tape the mural to the wall for display. Continue selecting different Bible stories each week until the class has worked its way to the end of the paper. After the completed mural has been on display for a while, cut the stories apart and give one section to each child to take home.

His Banner Over Me Is Love

This idea will give kids a fun project to work on for several weeks as well as help them to feel involved in the life of the whole congregation. Provide burlap, felt, glue, and scissors (or other supplies you'd like to use), and have kids create worship banners to hang in the church's worship area. Contact your pastor to find out what themes would be good ones to use.

Vitamin of the Day

As we're helping children grow spiritually, it's a good idea to help them grow physically as well. Make a list of the essential vitamins—you'll find these on the label of a multipurpose vitamin bottle. Match each vitamin with a different child. On the same day, send home an introductory letter to parents explaining that you would like each child to find out why our bodies need the vitamin matched to each child. Set up a schedule for a different vitamin to be studied each week. At the end of each class, one child should briefly explain why his or her vitamin is important for building and maintaining a strong, healthy body. After each explanation, a food rich in the specific vitamin can be passed around to the class as the snack for the day. For example, if calcium is the vitamin of the day, you might serve cheese slices. (Be sure to ask children about food allergies and provide other snacks if needed.) Point out to kids that God wants us to take care of our bodies, and he gives us many different resources, including the food we eat, to help us.

Cooking Club

Encourage consistent attendance by organizing a weekly "cooking" session. Each week, assign a different child the honor of selecting a no-bake recipe to plan and prepare for the rest of the class. At the beginning of a new season or quarter, set up an alternating schedule for each child to lead a short cooking lesson. Each child should be responsible for choosing a recipe with his or her parents' assistance, bringing in the ingredients, and demonstrating the how to's of making the treat. Send home explanatory notes to parents detailing the guidelines for this activity and the class schedule. Children will look forward to coming each week to share in the fun of experimenting with food and sampling the fresh goodies.

Children's Choir

Many churches have children's choirs that rehearse and sing during church services on a regular basis. If your church has such a choir, encourage the children in your Sunday school class to join it. If this opportunity doesn't exist in your church, consider starting a children's choir. Singing in a choir is a great experience for kids, and they'll be more likely to become involved in other programs in the church (including Sunday school). Also, their parents are sure to attend to see their little darlings sing!

Fundraising Fun

Have kids work together to design and implement a long-term fundraiser. Have kids decide what they want to raise funds for, such as buying new toys for the church nursery or sending Bibles overseas, and help them decide on a realistic goal. Let kids decide if they want the fundraiser to include just the members of their class, members of other classes, or the whole church. Have children create posters to generate excitement, and create a large "thermometer" on poster board to show their weekly progress. Celebrate with a party when they've reached their goal and have presented the money or the gifts.

It's a Wrap!

Kids are natural hams, so take advantage of that fact by making a class movie. At the beginning of the church year, borrow the church's video camera (or use your own) to begin your movie. Let kids introduce themselves, and tell a little bit about themselves. Then, periodically throughout the year, videotape kids during activities, games, songs, plays, parties, and so on. At the end of the year, have a party to present the movie. (Serve popcorn, of course!) You could even make a copy of the movie for each child in class as a special end-of-the-year surprise.

And don't forget—the movie would make a wonderful tool to help new kids feel welcome in class. Just send the movie home with the parents of the new child, and the newcomer will already feel connected. Then videotape the new child so he or she instantly becomes part of the group.

Create a Quilt

Have the kids in your class work together to create a quilt. Give each child several quilt squares and various craft materials to decorate with. Give kids time during every class to work on their quilt squares. When they're finished, sew the squares together (or find an able seamstress in your church to do it). Hang the quilt in your room, or donate it to an organization that can use it. There are several themes you could choose for the quilt. For example, kids could decorate their quilt squares to tell something about themselves. Or kids could make a "Jesus" quilt, in which each child decorates his or her quilt squares to tell about an event in Jesus' life.

My Church Needs Me

A good way to demonstrate the unity of the body of Christ is through service projects. Have kids form project teams of three or four, and ask each team to brainstorm and choose one service project idea that the whole class can be involved in. Some ideas might include helping elderly members of the church do their yardwork or taking homemade soup and sandwiches to the homeless. Give teams some guidelines, including the time frame for the project and a budget they have to work with. Have them think of everything that would be needed to complete the project, including necessary supplies, transportation, and other needs. When they're finished, have them present their ideas to the class. Then let the class vote on the order in which they'd like to do the projects. For each project, let the kids who thought of the idea act as leaders.

Note: Younger kids will need help figuring out logistics, but they can come up with some great ideas.

People Scavenger Hunt

Kids will be more likely to return to Sunday school (and church) if they feel that they have a connection with several people in the church. To help kids get to know more people in the church, have them go on a "People Scavenger Hunt." Use the "People Scavenger Hunt" handout (p. 56), or create your own that is more specific to your church membership. Give each child a handout, and encourage him or her to approach people in the church and have them sign the appropriate lines. You may want to announce this project in a church service and encourage church members to help kids get all the lines on their handouts signed. Give kids several weeks to complete this project and then have them share with one another what they discovered about the people in their church.

Prize Winners

Obtain items that kids would enjoy. These can be small, simple items, such as a new box of crayons or a package of bubble gum. Or, if you'd like, you can choose more elaborate items, such as movie tickets or T-shirts. You may be able to get businesses to donate items. Create an "entry box" by cutting a hole in the lid of a shoebox, and place a stack of scrap paper and pencils near the box. Show kids the items you have, and tell them that every time they attend Sunday school, they'll get to sign an entry form (and have one more chance to win!). At the end of the quarter, draw names out of the entry box and give away the prizes. Have enough prizes so that all kids can be winners.

A fun twist on this idea would be to have kids donate their own "white elephants"—toys, books, or videos that are in good condition that they don't want anymore—and hold a drawing for those items.

People Scavenger Hunt

1. Find three people who sing in a choir, and have them sign these lines: _____,

_____, _____.

2. Find a person who teaches a Sunday school class other than your own, and have him or her

sign here: _____.

3. Have a pastor or minister of your church sign here: _____.

4. Find a person who has been a member of your church for ten years or more, and have him or her

sign here: _____.

5. Find two people who play instruments in your church, and have them

sign here: _____, _____.

6. Find a person who helps to keep your church clean, and have him or her

sign here: _____.

7. Find a parent of one of your Sunday school classmates, and have him or her

sign here: _____.

8. Find two people who are members of a youth group in your church, and have them

sign here: _____, _____.

9. Find a person who helps take care of babies in the nursery during church, and have him or her

sign here: _____.

10. Find a person who greets people before church, and have him or her

sign here: _____.

Crafters' Corner

Kids love to make things! Create a crafters' corner in your classroom to encourage young crafters while helping them learn more about Bible times. Select several types of crafts that were found in Bible times, such as pottery and weaving. Find someone in your church who can lead children in doing these types of crafts, and help him or her purchase necessary supplies. Then, once a month, have a time designated to work on crafts. Have your helper show kids how to make Bible-time crafts while you share with them how these items were used in the Bible.

One great resource you can use is *Bible-Time Crafts Your Kids Will Love*, published by Group Publishing.

Writers' Journal

Showcase kids' writing talents by creating a class writers' journal. Think of a theme for the journal, and encourage kids to write poems and short stories about the theme. For example, you might have kids write about how they've seen God at work in their lives. Some kids might like to illustrate the stories and poems as well. After you have several submissions, have kids work together to "publish" the journal. These would make great Christmas presents for friends and family members!

Adopt a Child

Kids will enjoy working together to help a child who is less fortunate than they are. Work with an agency such as Compassion International or Christian Children's Fund. Let kids donate a few dollars apiece, or encourage them to hold a fundraiser to get money, and have the class sponsor a child. Kids can write letters and send cards to their sponsored child.

School Volunteers

A great way to stay connected with kids when they don't come to Sunday school is to volunteer as a playground or lunchroom monitor at a school. Pick the school most of your kids attend, or choose one in your neighborhood. You'll have the opportunity to get to know some kids better, to remind them that they're welcome at Sunday school, and to keep up with what's going on in their lives.

Parents Plus

nvolving parents and caregivers, as well as other members of the church and the community, is probably the best thing you can do to help build your attendance. Children are dependent on their parents to get them to Sunday school. If parents feel that their children are cared for and growing in a

Sunday school classroom, they're much more likely to make the effort to get kids there. They also really appreciate being involved in what's going on in your classroom. Another important idea is to help kids

forge relationships with other church members. This gives them a sense of belonging to a bigger "family." This section will provide you with some good ideas to help involve parents and the church as a whole in your program.

Classroom Carnival

Variety is a good way to increase interest in your program and boost attendance at the same time. Set aside a Sunday once in a while for a carnival day, and make sure to give it plenty of publicity. Then have your class set up a variety of Bible games and activities and invite another class to come to the carnival. Your carnival can be as simple or as elaborate as you and your class wish. For a real "blow-out," you can even ask parents to help create and run the games. Some game ideas include a fishing pond with small prizes, a Bible *Jeopardy!*-type game, and a Bible character dress-up relay. Let your imagination go wild!

Field Trips

Kids are very interested in what other denominations believe and the way they worship. Once a month, work with the parents of your children to take your class on a field trip to worship at another church. Be sure to prepare children ahead of time for what to expect, and make sure you have permission from parents. When you return, discuss things that were the same and different from your own church. This activity will help kids feel more of a connection with their own church as they understand more about the church's traditions and beliefs.

Parents' Corner

Help parents feel more involved in your program by providing them with their own space in your Sunday school room. This could be a wall, a shelf, or a table. Parents can use this space to express support and encouragement through symbols, letters, and pictures. This is also a good place for parents to sign up to bring refreshments, help with driving, or help with other programs.

Bible Day

Most churches give Bibles to children at some point during the kids' educational development. Create a special ceremony to involve children's parents in this special celebration. Have parents give the Bibles to their children as they say a few words about what the Bible means to them.

Who Am I?

Make a list of favorite Bible characters. Match each character on this list with a parent-child team. Send home a letter explaining the activity and assigning each team a date to present its character. Ask parents to come with their child to class and dress up like the Bible figure. The child and his or her parents should read about their character in the Bible and select a single event to act out for the class. Dressed in the person's attire, the parent and child should bring in any necessary props and silently act out their charade. Other children should sit quietly until the charade is over and then try to guess who the character might be.

Surprise Visitors

Keep kids on their toes and coming back to Sunday school by inviting a special visitor each week. The visitor should be a different person each time, although you could invent some recurring characters who make sporadic appearances. Be sure to keep the identity of the next week's visitor a secret, but remind kids to expect the unexpected!

Surprise visitors can help tell a Bible story, present an object lesson, introduce the week's topic, serve snacks, or just bring a smile to kids' faces. Recruit adults or youth in your church to be your surprise visitors. You could also recruit some people from the community to visit. Here are some ideas for surprise visitors: clowns, Bible characters, famous historical figures (especially from church history), animals, or goofy fictional characters. Some recurring characters might be a mad scientist, a clumsy police officer, or someone from another planet.

Intergenerational Fun!

Children's learning is impacted a great deal when they learn along with people of many different age groups. Try having an intergenerational class one Sunday a month. Together with other Sunday school teachers and your pastor, plan activities and events that will benefit and nourish the spiritual lives of all involved. Publicize this special class ahead of time, and encourage everyone to come and share in a fun time of fellowship. *Family Sunday School Fun* from Group Publishing is a great resource to use for intergenerational learning.

Feed Me!

Jesus fed his listeners with miraculously multiplied fish and bread. He understood the physical needs that must be met as a first step toward ministering to every area of a person's life. It's hard to fill a child's mind and heart with spiritual truth if his or her stomach is empty. One idea is to provide a family breakfast before classes begin on Sunday morning. The fellowship of a meal builds relationships and can result in a feeling of mutual accountability for regular attendance.

Progressive Meal

Visit kids at home to make them feel more comfortable and add a personal element to Sunday school. Plan a progressive meal with some of the families of the kids in your Sunday school class. Plan to eat each course of your meal at a different home. For example, you might start with salad at one home, move on to another home for bread, and so on. Ask each child's parents if they would like to host a course and help with the driving. Advertise this event ahead of time, and have each child pay several dollars toward the cost of the food. This is a great opportunity for kids to spend time in their friends' houses, and visiting and traveling together will help kids feel they're an important part of the group.

Adult Sharing Time

Help kids see that what they're learning in Sunday school now will have a positive impact on them their entire lives. Have a different child's parents come each week to share how much their childhood Sunday school experience means to them now.

Prayer Team

To help the children in your class feel loved and to help church members gain a deeper understanding of the ministry in your classroom, establish a children's prayer team. Invite people of every age to come a few minutes before class begins to pray for the children and that day's lesson. Ask these people to stay for a few minutes as class begins to welcome children by saying, "Hi, [name]! Welcome to Sunday school. We just prayed for you!" After the members of the prayer team leave, hang a sheet of newsprint on the wall of your meeting room and have children each write a prayer request on it. When the prayer team arrives the following week, show them the children's prayer requests to give them specific items to pray for.

Now Playing—Parents!

One sure way to keep kids involved in Christian education is to involve their parents. (After all, where the drivers go, the passengers must follow.) Make it a point to invite your kids' parents to your classroom on a regular basis. Everyone has a special skill— invite parents to "show off" a little! Maybe you have a musician in your midst, or an engineer, or a really great cook. Many adults think they have nothing to offer to children's ministry, but once they dip their feet in the water, you may find they're dedicated helpers.

Parent Conferences

Parents and children are used to parent-teacher conferences in secular settings. Put this idea to use in your classroom! After each quarter, schedule conferences with a few of your kids' parents.

You can schedule the conferences for before or after church, or you can set up other times to visit the families. By the end of the year, you'll have touched base with each of your kids' parents.

At each conference, discuss which Bible stories and truths you're teaching, evidence of spiritual growth you've noticed, and any concerns the parents may have. You can also use the conference to gain valuable information to help you become a better teacher. Ask what the children say at home about Sunday school and what Bible stories or lessons they seem to remember most.

You may even want to prepare a simple survey, such as the one on page 66, to send home with parents the week before their conference. Before you begin scheduling conferences, be sure to explain to kids the purpose of the meetings. Your goal isn't to judge each child, but to communicate with parents in order to form a team to promote spiritual growth and understanding.

Interviews

To help children feel more connected to their church family, have each child complete three interviews of people who aren't in your class. These interviews can be about any subject—good ideas might be Sunday school experiences or stories of when people came to know Christ. Help kids come up with good interview questions and have them practice interviewing one another. When they've completed their interviews, have them share the results with the class.

Have a Pageant!

As you know, many children love any kind of dramatic play including mime, role-play, and skits. If the children like it, chances are their parents do, too. Nearly every church has the traditional Christmas pageant, with cute kids dressed up like cows and sheep. Why not have other pageants or programs during the year?

Parent Survey

Thank you for taking the time to help me do a great job with your child. Please answer the following questions, and bring this survey with you when we meet.

1. How does your child feel about Sunday school?

_____

_____

2. What does your child say about what he or she is learning?

_____

_____

3. What spiritual growth have you seen in your child?

_____

_____

4. What Bible truths would you like to see your child learn?

_____

_____

5. Do you have suggestions for activities you would like us to do in class?

_____

_____

6. When could you be available to help in class?

_____

_____

7. Please list any other suggestions or concerns.

_____

_____

Utilize the acting skills and other abilities of parents and other adults in your church (include the kids, too) to put on a great show!

Meet and Greet

The more your students' parents know about you and your program, the more likely they'll be to encourage their children to attend. For this reason, among others, it's worth the time and expense to get to know your kids' parents. At the beginning of a new year—and whenever a new child joins your group—meet with each child's parents. Even if you have to rearrange your schedule a bit, do what you can to make the meetings as convenient for the parents as possible. If a child's parents work, for example, meet them before work for doughnuts, during breaks at work, or after work for coffee. Convey your excitement about the program and their child's involvement in it, and let them know what they can expect from you and the program. Most importantly, though, just use the time to get to know the parents and to let them get to know you.

Survey Says...

A survey is a quick, easy way to get to know parents' likes, dislikes, attitudes, and needs, and it helps them feel connected to your program. At the beginning of the year, send out an informal survey or questionnaire to the parents of every child on your class list. Provide a self-addressed, stamped envelope, and ask that the surveys be returned within a specified period of time. Some possible questions are listed below:

- What were your experiences in Sunday school like?
- What would you like your child to gain from coming to Sunday school?
- Would you like to share any special gifts or talents with us? What are they?

Parent Helpers

Involve children's parents in the program by asking them to take on special but simple responsibilities. First create a list of children's parents and plan to rotate responsibilities so all parents occasionally have a chance to be involved. Then brainstorm and write down a list of simple responsibilities, such as bringing snacks, helping in the classroom, reading Bible stories, leading songs, and so on. Be sure to include some responsibilities that parents who have to work on program days can achieve. Spend some time regularly brainstorming more ideas as you plan each program day. Contact children's parents personally; talk with them face to face if possible. Explain that you'd like them to be involved in what their children are doing and that you have several options for them to do so. Allow the parents to choose one or two options that work best for them, but don't push them if they say no. Then don't forget to remind parents a day or two before they need to fulfill their responsibility.

Parents' Day

Spend time each week working on a program for the children's parents. You may want to include a song or memory verses, or set up an art gallery displaying crafts and pictures created by your students. Have kids make invitations to welcome parents, grandparents, or special friends to the program. Children could make a banner by stamping handprints or footprints onto freezer paper. This program will give children an end project to work toward. It will also include parents or grandparents who may not be active in a church program themselves.

Take-Home Cards

On index cards or heavy paper, create take-home cards for each student. The cards should include two headings: "What I learned today" and "Something I did well." Before class, copy a one-sentence summary about the lesson under "What I learned today." Older children may add their own ideas to the summary. Throughout class time, write brief, encouraging notes to let parents know how their kids are doing in class. Send the cards home with students weekly to keep parents informed and to encourage parental involvement and support.

Clown Troupe

On a warm Saturday, send a group of church members to the park dressed as clowns. Clowns can go to several busy parks in your area or stick to one where families are likely to be. Arm the clowns with helium tanks, ribbon or string, and plenty of balloons. Clowns can inflate balloons and hand them out to children in the park. On each balloon, tie a card inviting children to attend your Sunday school program. Instruct the clowns to be sensitive to parents, making sure they don't seem to be approaching children in an inappropriate way.

Note: Be sure clowns go out in pairs or larger groups for safety reasons. This may also minimize any concerns parents might have about strangers talking to their children.

Community Carnival

Host a carnival at your church, and invite kids who attend to come to Sunday school. Consider holding this event toward the end of the summer or at another time when children are out of school and families are looking for something to do. You may want to start planning the event at least a year in advance, making sure it doesn't conflict with any other family event or children's event in the community. Ask the parents of your Sunday school students to help out. Publicize the event on community-events calendars, on local TV and radio stations, and through posters. Invite the entire community.

It's a good idea to invest some money in this event so it will be attractive to busy families. You may even want to hire a professional to plan and carry out the carnival. Invite parents and other church members to help out, but make sure they are well-trained and have a good understanding of the purpose of the event.

You'll need clowns, fun games, festive music, good prizes, and great food. At the carnival, invite children and their families to attend Sunday school. You may want to make brochures available with information about your church and its Sunday school program. Leave it at that, though. If people perceive that your church has tricked them into attending a high-pressure endorsement of your church, they'll be turned off from attending. Encourage the children and families in your church to attend so that others can get to know them.

Progressive Play

Encourage children who haven't been to your program for a while to return by holding a progressive "play date" about once a quarter. You'll need enough insured vehicles and drivers to hold all the children in your group. You'll also need to arrange a time and place for your children to play—Saturday afternoon or Sunday morning during class time, for example. Then you'll need to contact the parents of all the children you'd like to invite back to your program. Ask those parents if your students can drop by on the particular day and invite the children to play. On the play day, have all your kids climb into cars and have parents drive to each missing student's home. Encourage all the kids to sing a fun song as they walk to the door of the home. When the child comes to the door, have your students ask the child to come and play. After you've rounded up all the kids, head to a park or another fun location to play. After the play date, you'll need to drive the kids back to their homes. Be sure to have several children who regularly attend your program escort the other children back home and invite them to come to church again.

Sharing Sunday

You can increase interest as well as attendance by occasionally sharing an activity with another class. With enough people participating, you might even be able to share with the entire congregation. For example, for Palm Sunday, you can order palm leaves from the florist and make simple crosses for everyone attending the worship service. All you need to do is get two small pieces of palm leaf. Cut a small lengthwise slit in one of them and thread the other through the slit at a right angle, making a cross. Supply pins, and soon everyone will be wearing crosses made from palm leaves!

This Is Your Life!

A great way to recognize and celebrate a child in your program is to bring together as many of the people who are important to him or her as possible—parents, siblings, teachers, coaches, and friends. Have each person share why the child is important and special. If these people aren't able to get together, have them write letters or videotape their comments.

Great Grandparents!

C hildren benefit greatly from a close relationship with their grandparents. Unfortunately, many children are denied this relationship because their grandparents are no longer living or they live far away. Establish an "Adopt a Grandparent" program. Kids who would like to be "adopted" can be matched up with older adults who would love to act as "grandparents."

Grandparent-grandchild pairs can spend time together in structured programs you provide. This idea not only provides each child with one more adult who cares about him or her, but it also involves more adults in your program.

Ice Cream Social

Encourage family time while getting to know all of your students' families by hosting an ice cream social. Send out invitations ahead of time, asking each family to bring its favorite kind of ice cream, enough for about six people. Provide necessary utensils and serving dishes, as well as various kinds of toppings. Families will enjoy eating sundaes together! A fun variation might be to give awards for the biggest sundae and the most unusual sundae. Encourage each family to bring along friends who aren't regular churchgoers.

Family Devotion

This is a great idea for older students! Have kids work in teams to create family devotion books. Provide each team with sample devotions, books of stories or quotes, Bibles, concordances, and a theme. Be sure that kids know the elements to be included in each devotion, such as a Bible passage, a story or quote, and discussion questions. When teams have finished their work, bind the devotions together in a booklet and mail one to each family. Encourage family members to share in the devotions together.

Creative Communication

It's always fun to get mail, but kids especially love it. There are many different ways of communicating how wonderful your Sunday school program is, and the more often you communicate with kids and their parents, the better your relationships will be. The ideas in this section will ensure your communication always follows the three F's: Friendly, Fun, and Frequent.

Take-Home Fun

Whenever possible, let children take home something that reminds them of what they learned about the Bible. This might be a picture the child drew, a take-home paper with reminders of the Bible story, or a fun craft. Children are more likely to share what they learned if they have an item to tell about. Parents will bring their children back to a place where their children learn and remember Bible events.

Piece by Piece

To illustrate the important role of each child in your class, cut a piece of poster board into puzzle pieces and write the name of one student on each piece. The overall shape of the puzzle can be a person, a church building, or a simple geometric shape. Mail one piece to each child at the beginning of the week, with instructions to bring the piece to Sunday school the following Sunday. Assemble the pieces in class, and talk about how important each piece is to making the puzzle complete. Encourage children to name specific skills and contributions each person brings to class.

Bookmarks

At the beginning of the year, purchase a small stack of bookmarks at a local Christian bookstore. Mail these out to your kids every so often to spark excitement and to remind them of Sunday school. If you'd like, you can send out blank bookmarks with an invitation to kids to decorate them and bring them in to show to the class. Better yet, suggest that kids give the bookmarks to friends and invite their friends to Sunday school.

Cardboard Cutouts

Obtain some large cardboard boxes (the type refrigerators or stoves might be packed in). Create cardboard cutouts of Bible characters, and cut holes where the faces would be. Involve kids in "dressing" these characters and making them look real. Take a picture of each child with his or her face in the cut-out space. Save these and send the pictures to kids from time to time—especially those who might have missed a week or two. Children get a kick out of seeing themselves in funny poses, and the simple reminder of the Bible characters will help keep kids actively learning and growing.

Singspiration

You'll need a tape recorder and a blank tape for this activity. Invite kids to write their own class theme song. This song should reflect the good feelings and attitudes the class tries to promote. The song could be sung to a popular tune or a television theme song. It could even be performed as a rap. Once kids have recorded the song, make copies and send the tapes to absent kids or to those who are potential class members.

Subscription Prescription

There are now dozens of Christian magazines for children. Many of these have lower rates when several subscriptions are purchased at once. At the beginning of the year, purchase subscriptions for the kids in your class and send cards announcing the gifts. This will generate initial excitement for kids and their parents and will provide quality reading material.

Post Office

To encourage kids to be at Sunday school every week, set up a post office in your classroom. On a board or a wall, attach envelopes with a child's name printed on the outside of each one. Let kids write encouraging notes to one another during class and place the notes in the envelopes. You can also write notes to kids, encouraging them to be in Sunday school, lifting them up when they are experiencing hard times, praising them for jobs well done, and offering help in times of need. At the end of each class, children may take home their mail.

Awesome Advertising

Take out an ad in your local newspaper to invite kids to your Sunday school program. Many newspapers will donate ad space or reduce the prices for church groups. Put the ad in a place where kids or their parents are likely to see it, such as near the comics or the school news. Be sure to include fun, kid-friendly graphics and a few things about upcoming events and study topics.

Face to Face

When it comes to communication, often good old-fashioned, face-to-face contacts are best. Kids love to have the undivided attention of an adult, even if it's just for a short period of time. Make it a goal to make an appointment with each of the children on your class list at least once during the year. Take the child out for ice cream or to play in the park—anything the child would like to do. Make sure the activity is OK with the child's parents, and allow the child to bring a friend along if that would make him or her feel more comfortable. Talk with the child about what's important to him or her, and be sure to invite the child to get (or stay!) actively involved in Sunday school.

Note: To ensure appropriate appearances, be sure to meet in a public place.

Class Calendar

Create a monthly class calendar to keep kids (and parents) informed about class news and activities. Include on your calendar important class events such as field trips, birthdays, and special projects.

Let kids help design the calendars by drawing illustrations or messages to include each month. For example, they might draw pictures of Bible stories they've been studying, or they might write favorite Bible verses or truths they've learned. Then use a copy machine to reduce the drawings or sayings to a small enough size to use on the calendar. You may even want to include short activities for families to do together at home to strengthen their faith or to just get them talking.

Send the calendars home with the children, or mail them directly to the parents. Also keep copies of the calendars in your classroom, and provide one to your Christian education director or church office.

What's Coming Up?

To build excitement for an upcoming Sunday school lesson, send out "What's coming up?" announcements. After you teach your Sunday school lesson, spend a few minutes looking over next week's lesson. Pick out some key activities or ideas that you know your children will enjoy. Then create a small flier with the words "Things you don't want to miss!" at the top, and illustrate the fun activities underneath. Make your program sound fun and exciting so kids will want to attend. You can mail these fliers once a quarter, every month, or even each week.

Wanted!

A unique way to remind absent children that they are missed is to make creative "Wanted!" posters. Invite an artistically inclined church member to sketch some humorous faces. Arrange these on a poster with some friendly words of encouragement or praise such as "Wanted in class this Sunday! You are missed, pardner!" Send these out to kids who have missed a few Sundays.

Prayer Chain

If you have a group of older kids, consider establishing a prayer chain. Photocopy the "Prayer Chain" handout (p. 81) or make your own. List children's names and phone numbers, and put your name in the first link. Make copies of the prayer chain, and ask kids to place the lists near their phones. Tell kids that whenever there's a prayer request from any member in the group, they need to call you first and you'll call the person listed after you. Then that person must call the next person. When kids get a prayer request phone call, they should call the person listed after them and then stop and pray for the person in need.

Prayer Chain

Parent Letter

To help parents keep up with missed classes and to help children who miss classes keep up and feel welcome after being gone, type up and photocopy the lessons you'll be covering throughout the month or quarter. Mail them to each parent along with a letter like the following:

Dear Parents,

We know that now and then you'll be away from your home church and your children will be unable to attend Sunday school. Because Christian education is vitally important to their faith development, we're sending you the upcoming Sunday school topics. If your children have to miss a class, you can use these topics to help them catch up. You can also use these lessons to help deepen what they're learning in class. Consider researching each topic and discussing it with your children.

We love your children. Thank you for letting us be a part of their spiritual development and growth in Jesus.

Sincerely,

_____

(Sunday school teacher)

That's Affirmative!

Get some postcards, and write one of the following verses on each postcard: Hebrews 10:24; 1 Thessalonians 1:2; 1 Corinthians 13:13; and 1 Corinthians 16:13. Pass them out to the class at the beginning of each month and invite students to send the cards to friends who are feeling down or are going through difficult times. Continue this tradition throughout the year and you'll see a marked increase in attendance and in the spirit of your class.

Self Postcards

If they're not in the habit of attending church and Sunday school, some kids may forget. Since most kids enjoy receiving mail, have them each spend time in class writing a postcard to themselves. They can write a note to themselves telling why they should return. Then the card could be passed around so that other kids have the opportunity to write an encouraging note on the card reminding the child to come back. Mail the card so it will arrive on Friday or Saturday.

Photo Cards

If you regularly take photographs of your class in action, you know that there are usually four or five really good pictures from each roll of film and a lot of so-so pictures. But have you ever noticed that photographs are similar in size to postcards? Try using those good-but-not-great pictures to boost class attendance by writing a message on the back of each one and sending the photos to children who have missed a Sunday or two. Kids will enjoy seeing some of the activities your class is doing, and they may decide that they don't want to miss out on the fun!

Unique Birthday Cards

Generate a chronological birthday list of the children in your class. About a week before each birthday, have all the kids except the one whose birthday is coming up sign a card with a line about why they like the birthday child. Let this be a mock secret— the birthday child knows a card will be signed for him or her but can pretend not to see the others signing it. Send the card to the birthday child to arrive on the big day.

We're Glad You Came!

Have kids make and decorate a batch of postcards that say "We're glad you came!" Then in random order, perhaps by drawing names, send two each week to children who were in class. Kids will want to come to see who they get to send the cards to. If children bring their cards with them the following week, you might allow them to draw the next two names.

Newsworthy

If the newspaper in your city covers school events, read the paper carefully and watch for news about your students. Each time one of your children is mentioned, cut out the article, highlight that child's name, and mail it to him or her with your words of pride. Encourage children to let you know when a classmate is in the paper. Emphasize "classmate" so the child who points out the article shines by showing another's accomplishments.

Baby Bonus

In infant and toddler classes, take a minute or two to write a note to the parents of each child and send the note home in the diaper bag. Tell the parents about something cute or funny their child did, an activity the whole class enjoyed, or something new the child learned. Write each note in first person, as though the preschooler wrote it. Here's an example:

Dear Mom and Dad,

Today we played with clay. I shared my clay very nicely. I slept for about thirty minutes. Thanks for bringing me to Sunday school.

Love,
Becky

Parents will want to bring their children to a church where their children receive such personalized attention.

Preview Fun

When you're having children or their parents fill out information forms at the beginning of the year, be sure to ask for e-mail addresses. Then, each Friday or Saturday, compose an e-mail message that gives a question or a "teaser" about Sunday's lesson. Send this to each child. For children whose families don't have e-mail, mail a note to arrive on Friday or Saturday.

"I Like You" Call

Phone three children per week just to tell each one why you like him or her. Don't wait until they miss a Sunday to do this. Make sure to call everyone by the end of a quarter. Here's an example of what you might say:

"Hi, Michael. This is Mr. Williams. I called to say I like you. One of the reasons I like you is that you smile in a way that encourages others in the class. Thanks for helping them feel at home. I'll see you on Sunday!"

Note: Leave messages if children are not home. Not only will they hear your affirmation, but parents will as well.

Phone Question

Kids love answering the phone, especially if the person on the other end wants to talk just to them! Tell kids that you'll be calling them sometime during the next week with a Bible question. Then call each one, leaving voice mail messages for kids who aren't at home. Ask a question about the Bible passage you will study next or about the one you just studied. Give the child time to find the answer in his or her Bible, and then congratulate him or her for the effort. If you must leave a voice-mail message, suggest that children come up with a question about that same passage, perhaps with their parents' help, and call you back. Promise to answer the question on Sunday if they call you when you're not home.

Mail for Me?

Children very seldom get their own mail, so a regular letter from church is a special treat. Send mail to all your students at least once a month. Don't make them miss a Sunday to hear from you. Some ideas for notes you might send are listed below:

- A brief note about the topic the class just studied, along with a way the child demonstrates some aspect of that topic. For example, you might write, "On Sunday, we studied compassion. I like that you are considerate of the feelings of the people in your family and school."
- A note to tell the child why he or she is wonderful. For example, you might write, "You're wonderful because you help people feel at home."
- A note to tell the child about the upcoming topic and to ask him or her to bring or prepare something for class. For example, you might write, "This coming Sunday, we'll be studying families. Will you bring a picture of your family or plan to tell us what you like about your family?"

Fun Holidays

Remind kids that you're thinking about them as well as encouraging them to come to Sunday school by making and sending your own greeting cards for unusual holidays, such as Universal Children's Day (November 20), National Ice Cream Day (July 16), or Mother Goose Day (May 18).

"We Love You!" Packages

If a child in your Sunday school class has an extended illness or is injured and misses Sunday school for a long period of time, have the class create a "We Love You!" care package to send or deliver to the child. Encourage kids to bring in items that will remind the recipient of every student in class. Include positive, cheerful notes and other things the child might enjoy, such as coloring books, a favorite treat, and small toys.

We Miss You!

To let children know they are missed when they're not able to make it to Sunday school, spend a few minutes of each class session having children write to kids who are absent. Make several photocopies on heavy paper of the "We Miss You!" card (page 89) and keep them in your classroom. When a child is absent, pass the card around the room and have children each write a short note to the child who's missing. If the children in your class are very young, have them draw pictures on the card or help them write their names. After class, mail the card to the child who was absent.

We Miss You!

Wherever you are...

Whatever you're doing...

Our hearts are aching...

Because *you* aren't here!

Address Labels

Regularly print out adhesive address labels for every child on your class list. Then stick these on postcards. Keep this stack of pre-addressed cards with you and write a few anytime you have some spare minutes, such as during your lunch hour, while you sit in a traffic jam, or while you're waiting in the doctor's office. Bits of time add up to significant attention, attention which children translate as, "My church cares about me."

Using address labels makes certain you send the same number of mail pieces to each child. You won't favor either those who attend, or those who don't attend, and you won't send postcards just to the kids you know best. When you finish one stack, print and attach another set of labels to postcards.

Picture This!

For nonreaders or children who are just starting to read, send your postcards or your mail in rebus form, using pictures to represent words. You might send them a Bible verse you want them to remember or an invitation to next week's Sunday school. Change as many words of the verse or sentence into pictures as you can.

For example, "Do not let the sun go down while you are still angry" (Ephesians 4:26b) could be drawn like this:

Do not let the ☼ go ⬇
while U R still ☹.

Coded Messages

Children love secret code, so send them a coded message that relates to the lesson you'll be studying the coming Sunday. Ask them to bring you the solution to the message on Sunday. Have extras to give visitors who may not have received the coded message. Here's a sample:

- Put lines between the words to read this verse that we'll study on Sunday:

THENYOUWILLUNDERSTANDWHATISRIGHTANDJUSTANDFAIREVERYGOODPATHPROVERBS2:9

Riddle Me This

Send riddles about the coming lesson, promising the children that you'll give the answers when they come on Sunday. Riddles can come in several forms (see the following samples).

- **Who or what am I?** "I'm the animal feeding box in which Jesus was laid. I was Jesus' first bed." (Find the answer in Luke 2:7.)
- **Rhyming** "I said Mary was highly favored.
  Then she felt a little troubled;
  So I told her not to be afraid.
  Then to God she prayed."
  (Find the answer in Luke 1:26-38, 46.)
- **Simple question** "Who was Jesus' cousin?" (Find the answer in Luke 1:62-63.)

Nifty Newsletters

Your church newsletter or Web page can become a wonderful attendance-building tool with a little effort. First be sure to include the addresses of all your kids, as well as children who have visited, on the church's newsletter mailing list. Then spend some time reaching out to both your students and their parents through the newsletter. In each issue, include a personal note to the parents. Then add a quote from a parenting magazine, an uplifting Scripture, an easy family devotion, a fun family activity, or a note of encouragement to weary parents. You'll want to be sensitive to parents who aren't Christians or who aren't members of your church; avoid Christian jargon, for example. Include material just for the kids too. Get kids excited about your program: Tell them something fun you're planning for the next class, ask them a riddle that they'll be able to answer after the following class, or suggest an activity for kids to do with their parents to review the previous week's lesson or to preview the coming week's lesson.

Quiz Cards

Think of a quiz question from the weekly lesson material covered in class. Write the question on the backs of postcards to be sent to children during the week. Include a phone number so kids can call to report their answers. The following Sunday, congratulate all who answered the question correctly. The weekly postcards will remind children of lesson material and encourage regular attendance.

Video Postcards

Here's a way to stay connected to kids when they don't come to Sunday school. Have a volunteer take some videotape of your Sunday school class. Be sure the tape shows children having fun and participating in a variety of activities. Then copy the videotape and send a copy to each child who hasn't been to Sunday school in a while. Include a colorful note, card, or postcard with a warm invitation to come to Sunday school.

Better yet, hand-deliver the videotapes to kids' homes. You

may even want to bring one or two children with you to make the deliveries. No matter how you deliver the tapes, be sure to avoid making children feel guilty for not attending Sunday school or making them think you're angry with them. Show them who Jesus is by letting them know you love them!

Quick Personalization

When a significant Sunday is coming, send an invitation to each child on your class list. To make this both personal and quick, compose the message on your computer's labelmaking feature. Pick a fun font that children will enjoy, and print in color if possible. Then print out as many copies as you need on 2x4-inch laser labels. Stick the labels on the center of the message side of postcards. Then add your signature and a line of personal greeting. This gives the speed of printed material with the personalization of your handwriting. For an idea, see the following sample.

Hey wonderful sixth-graders!

I just wanted to remind you that we are starting our unit on "Nobodies of the New Testament" this Sunday. We'll discover that everybody is somebody when he or she does what God asks. These little-known Bible characters are big heroes, just like you can be. Come find out how. I can't wait to learn about Jesus with you.

I'm looking forward to seeing you Sunday, Michael!

Love in Christ,
Mrs. Johnson
